BLACKHEATH
A THIRD SELECTION

ANTHONY H. PAGE

SUTTON PUBLISHING

Sutton Publishing Limited
Phoenix Mill · Thrupp · Stroud
Gloucestershire · GL5 2BU

First published 2007

Copyright © Anthony H. Page, 2007

Title page photograph: Blackheath Market
Place in the early 1960s. *(Eunice Dudley)*

British Library Cataloguing in Publication Data
A catalogue record for this book is available from the
British Library.

ISBN 978-0-7509-4705-3

Typeset in 10.5/13.5 Photina.
Typesetting and origination by
Sutton Publishing Limited.
Printed and bound in England by
J.H. Haynes & Co. Ltd, Sparkford.

*I would like to dedicate this book to Janet Kathleen Page (1947–2003),
without whose help, support and encouragement none of my books would have
been completed.*

THE BLACK COUNTRY SOCIETY

The Black Country Society is proud to be associated with
Sutton Publishing of Stroud. In 1994 the society was
invited by Sutton Publishing to collaborate in what has
proved to be a highly successful publishing partnership,
namely the extension of the ***Britain in Old Photographs***
series into the Black Country. In this joint venture the Black
Country Society has played an important role in establishing and developing a
major contribution to the region's photographic archives by encouraging society
members to compile books of photographs of the area or town in which they live.

The first book in the Black Country series was *Wednesbury in Old Photographs* by
Ian Bott, launched by Lord Archer of Sandwell in November 1994. Since then
almost 70 Black Country titles have been published. The total number of
photographs contained in these books is in excess of 13,000, suggesting that the
whole collection is probably the largest regional photographic survey of its type in
any part of the country to date.

This voluntary society was founded in 1967 as a reaction to the trends of the
late 1950s and early '60s. This was a time when the reorganisation of local
government was seen as a threat to the identity of individual communities and
when, in the name of progress and modernisation, the industrial heritage of the
Black Country was in danger of being swept away.

The general aims of the society are to stimulate interest in the past, present and
future of the Black Country, and to secure at regional and national levels an
accurate understanding and portrayal of what constitutes the Black Country and,
wherever possible, to encourage and facilitate the preservation of the Black
Country's heritage.

The society, which now has over 2,500 members worldwide, organises a yearly
programme of activities. There are six venues in the Black Country where evening
meetings are held on a monthly basis from September to April. In the summer
months, there are fortnightly guided evening walks in the Black Country and its
green borderland, and there is also a full programme of excursions further afield by
car. Details of all these activities are to be found on the society's website,
www.blackcountrysociety.co.uk, and in ***The Blackcountryman***, the quarterly
magazine that is distributed to all members.

PO Box 71 · Kingswinford · West Midlands DY6 9YN

CONTENTS

An aerial view over the town, with the railway line crossing diagonally from the top right-hand corner, before entering the tunnel at the bottom left, with the churchyard of St Paul's Church just below it. (*Author's Collection*)

INTRODUCTION

'Change and decay in all around I see.'

This line from the well-known hymn, 'Abide with Me', could well describe the sentiments of many people when making a visit to the once thriving town centre of Blackheath. The last decade has seen tremendous change, if not decay, in many aspects of the topography of the district, with the disappearance of schools, industrial concerns, small businesses and housing stock, all in the name of progress. In common with similar towns up and down the country, whenever a plot of land becomes available, new housing stock appears at an amazing rate, and visitors who have not been here for a couple of years will find the landscape changed beyond recognition.

At the time of writing, the latest change has been the completion of the last stage of the ring road, built to ease congestion around the Market Place and High Street. The only problem is that motorists have not yet taken to it, and so the benefits are still to be seen.

The loss of many well-established large manufacturing industries, often the source of employment for whole families, has meant that the face of the population is changing too, with people having to move out of the place which has been home to previous generations in order to seek either work or further education.

But all is not doom and gloom. The interest in things past and the heritage revival continues apace, as is shown by the ever-increasing membership of the Local History Group and attendances at its meetings; the support of local newspapers in publishing items of nostalgic concern also reflects a proud connection with days gone by.

In this volume it is hoped that the reader will be able to identify with the places, people and events portrayed. Many of the pictures will have a good deal of information, some will not, and if anyone has any additions or corrections to make the author will be pleased to have them.

Anthony H. Page

High Street Methodist Church just before demolition in 1996. *(Sheila Brookes)*

1

Street Scenes

The top of High Street at the junction with Holly Road in the early part of the twentieth century, looking towards the town centre. On the left the business premises of John Tooth are still part of the family residence. *(Ken Rock Collection)*

The Handel Hotel lies empty as it awaits demolition, together with the other properties visible in Birmingham Road, mid-1970s. In preparation for the new traffic flow system, Oldbury Road has been closed to traffic. *(Ron Wood)*

The Handel Hotel, together with the other properties at the top of Oldbury Road, has recently been demolished, and the fencing is in place preparatory to the building of the Kwik-Save food store, late 1970s. On the extreme right is the Halesowen and Hasbury Co-op store. *(CHAS)*

Taken from the top of Gorsty Hill this picture looks towards High Haden on the skyline, with the post office (closed in 2005) in the centre. It dates from the mid-1980s. *(Ivan Pitchford)*

West Street links Heath Street with John Street, and here we can see the Bible Hall on the extreme right, mid-1980s. The wall and trees in the distance are the garden of the large house in Beeches Road, once home to the local doctor, and later used as the vicarage for Holy Trinity Church, Old Hill. *(CHAS)*

There are not too many passengers waiting at Rowley Regis & Blackheath station in this picture, dating from the 1920s, which is looking in the direction that the train will travel towards Snow Hill station, Birmingham. *(Author's Collection)*

The Coronation Club in Park Street is seen just before it was demolished in 2005 to make way for the final section of the ring road. The club was relocated on Oldbury Road. *(Geoffrey Moore)*

A typical back garden of one of the council houses in Habberley Road, together with the Anderson shelter which has not yet been taken down, even though the war has been over for about five years. *(Gwen Davies)*

Although this postcard, which dates from the early 1920s, is entitled Market Place, it is a view taken from Halesowen Street looking in the direction of Oldbury Road. On the extreme right is the California public house, one of the few still trading under the same name and looking rather unchanged to the

present day (see page 39). Next to it is Connop's drapers shop and the Royal Oak public house, opposite which is The Shambles. *(Ken Rock Collection)*

A 1929 photograph which is inscribed 'The camping ground, Hill and Cakemore'. It is believed to have been taken in Station Road (now Nimmings Road), and was the area reserved for travellers passing through the area. *(Author's Collection)*

A similar view to that on page 12, but dating from slightly later, shows that the Midland Bank has now been constructed, and the hoarding over The Shambles is advertising the latest film to be shown at the Kings Cinema. *(Bob Grosvenor)*

From the Market Place looking up High Street, with O. Hobbs & Son, General Dealers, on the corner of Halesowen Street, early 1950s. Although few of the traders remain, the general façade of the buildings has altered little with the passing of time. *(CHAS)*

Darby Street from its junction with Beeches Road, winter 1986. The tower of High Street Methodist Church can be seen in the distance. Shortly after this picture was taken the whole street was demolished to make way for modern dwellings, most of which were constructed by the Black Country Housing Association, whose headquarters are situated opposite the church in High Street. *(CHAS)*

George Avenue, still known to many by its previous name of Mott Street, as seen from the corner with Birmingham Road, *c.* 1978. The corner shop is owned by Mr and Mrs Bonner, dealing both as a photographers and as a pram and baby goods supplier. Graham Bonner went on to become chief photographer at the *County Express*, Stourbridge. *(CHAS)*

A rare view of the corner of Malt Mill Lane and Long Lane, dating from the early 1920s, before the building of the commercial properties now occupying the right-hand side of the road. It appears to have been taken on Whit Monday, as the crowd gathering in the centre are displaying the Sunday School banner, suggesting they were on their way to the Annual Treat. *(Bob Grosvenor)*

Once described as the development that would take Blackheath into the next century, providing the town's first large supermarket and multi-storey car park, the Highshore Centre ran into financial difficulties and was abandoned before it could be finished. Here we see the demolition of the partly completed project, which was situated in Birmingham Road, in 1979. (*Anthony Page*)

The residential estate known as Regis Heath was built on land-fill on the site of the former Regis Brick Works in Oldbury Road. This picture shows how close it was to the LPG storage facility run by the Shell Company, before the latter ceased trading in the mid-1980s and the removal of the tanks. (*Anthony Page*)

An aerial view of Oldbury Road and district, *c.* 1920. The Salvation Army Citadel in Park Street is at the bottom left-hand corner, next to Price's Custard factory, with the houses on the other side of Park Street backing on to the Globe Manufacturing Company. The houses at the top left are Mott Street (now George Avenue) and Oldbury Road, with the Railway Inn and George Mason's garage. In the right foreground is Blackheath's first Picture Palace. The land at the top right was then allotments, but now contains the council housing in Spring Avenue and Habberley Road. (*Clarence Siviter*)

A further view of the bottom of High Street, this one dating from the 1970s. Hobbs's shop has been demolished to make the corner with Halesowen Street more open to improve visibility for the drivers of the increasing traffic. The fencing at the left of the picture marks the entrance to the infamous subway and toilets, used as underground shelters during the Second World War. *(Gordon Carter)*

We are looking down Causeway from the High Street end in this picture, dated 15 June 1969. The spire of Birmingham Road Methodist Church (often known locally as Causeway Chapel) is visible in the background, and the old cottages which used to stand on the extreme right have been taken down. *(CHAS)*

This old corn mill was transformed into a workshop by Mr Downing, and was situated behind the wool shop run by his wife in Halesowen Street. The picture dates from 1980. *(Robert Downing)*

The Travellers Rest public house surrounded by contractor's scaffolding is awaiting demolition in February 1997 to make way for the development of the ring road. The photograph is taken from outside the Britannia Building Society in Avenue Road; the Ashley Hotel is visible on the right. Shortly afterwards the entrance to Horner Way and thence to Sainsbury's car park will have replaced the buildings on the left. (*Ann Willetts*)

This early twentieth-century postcard of Long Lane, looking from the Quinton end towards Blackheath, shows the old rows of cottages. (*Author's Collection*)

A 1969 view of the junction of Causeway and Birmingham Road with South Staffs (previously Harpers) Garage on the right and the Methodist Church on the left. The garage was shortly afterwards demolished to make way for a sheltered housing complex. *(CHAS)*

The Falcon Works of Issachar Gadd, the makers of forgings and bolts among other things, situated in Beeches Road. This photograph was taken on 19 August 1972. *(CHAS)*

These old terraced cottages in George Avenue are awaiting demolition in May 1969. We are looking up towards Birmingham Road from outside the rear entrance to Hadley's Coaches and the Telephone Exchange. *(CHAS)*

Perry Park Road, commonly referred to as 'The Tump' (not to be confused with Tump Road, the old name for Beeches Road), is the curved road on the right. It was constructed to make the ascent of the trams from Old Hill to Blackheath an easier option than an attempt to use the much steeper Waterfall Lane. As can be seen it follows the railway line, which is entering the tunnel at the bottom of the picture, viewed here in winter 1976. *(Eric Parkes)*

The works van belonging to the Orchard sweet factory is parked outside their headquarters in Holly Road. Orchard Confectionery was well known around the Black Country, and was owned and run by members of the Willetts family, whose main business was in High Street. *(Malcolm Whitehouse)*

A derelict workshop in George Avenue, which had been constructed in 1904, is one of the last properties to be left standing during the redevelopment of the area in the late 1970s. At the extreme left of the picture is the Telephone Exchange in Oldbury Road, with an electricity sub-station between the two. The property now known as Regis Lodge, built as an elderly people's dwelling, currently offices of Sandwell Social Services, occupies the site. *(Ron Wood)*

The row of old houses situated on the corner of Holly Road and Powke Lane, 1969. The wall on the right is the boundary of the playground of Powke Lane Junior and Infant School, and the whole area is now transformed into a new housing complex. *(CHAS)*

These cottages, dating from the seventeenth century, stood opposite the camping ground seen on page 14 in Nimmings Road until they were demolished in about 1980. *(David Westwood)*

The last row of shops in Oldbury Road just before the whole area was cleared in 1979. The ones still open for business at this stage were Fred Hiscocks, Hayley Bearings, Horace Perks barber's shop (note the red and white symbol above the door), and the Railway public house. *(David Westwood)*

The tram tracks, which terminated just a few yards to the right of the picture, can be seen in this view of the High Street, taken in the mid-1920s. *(Author's Collection)*

2

Shops & Pubs

Displaying some of their fine range of products, the staff of T.P. Moyle waits cheerfully for customers, 1950s. One of several grocery shops in the High Street, Moyle's was one of a chain of shops which traded under that name throughout the southern part of the Black Country. (*Josie Rose*)

Mrs Jerry Westwood, seen in the early 1920s on the doorstep of the fish and chip shop which she ran with her husband. It occupied a prime position next to the Market Place. *(Colin Pratt)*

Bramwell Bryant stands outside his bicycle shop in Oldbury Road, late 1940s. When these premises were demolished he moved to other shops in Birmingham Road and High Street. As well as all things connected with cycling he also supplied electrical parts. Originally a member of the Salvation Army he was also associated with the Methodist Church, and in later life played the drums at numerous social activities. *(Florrie Webster)*

Gordon and Reg Carter opened their electronics business in Halesowen Street, and as business expanded they moved into this shop on High Street, which had previously been the newsagent and printing premises of Parkes Brothers. They were one of the foremost suppliers to the increasing demand for popular records in the 1960s, and also pioneered the rental television trade, expanding later into fancy goods. The picture dates from about 1970. *(Gordon Carter)*

The ladies' hairdressing premises of Maggie Sherwood in the Market Place, pictured on 12 April 1948, with Jean Parsons on the right of this group of workers. *(Susan Poston)*

The first major national store to open in Blackheath in the 1930s was Woolworths, which has continued to occupy the same position in High Street up to the present day, with only minor changes to the façade. Here we see it as it was in May 1986. *(Ned Williams)*

Annie Davenport is posing outside her drapery shop at the Shell corner in Long Lane, *c.* 1912 to 1915. With her are her children Mary Clay (from her first marriage) and Stephen and Rhoda. *(Margaret Carter)*

Riley's Optical Service and Drug Stores in the High Street, standing adjacent to the post office, in a picture taken in the early 1980s. It is a long-established business, which also had a branch at Shell Corner. It is still trading today. *(Ned Williams)*

A festive display graces the windows of Cramar Flowers in Halesowen Street, almost opposite the California public house, in this 1980s picture. *(Ned Williams)*

This magnificent display of meat and game hung outside the High Street shop of Eley's butchers, 1920s. There are sides of beef, ducks, geese, rabbits and hares clearly visible, while the notice says that three prime pigs are shortly to be slaughtered. *(Malcolm Whitehouse)*

Mrs Maria Willetts stands on the doorstep of Willetts & Sons, High Class Confectioners, opposite the George & Dragon at 59 High Street, 1920s. The business was initiated by Samuel Willetts, who was a master sugar-boiler, winning many national prizes for his artistic sugar sculptures, and for pioneering the technique of putting letters in sticks of rock. *(Dorothy Parkes)*

The Halesowen & Hasbury Cooperative Society Foodmarket, branch No. 4, in Oldbury Road, seen here in the early 1960s, stood opposite the junction with Summer Road. The shop now trades as Road Runner Motor Spares. *(Ned Williams)*

Priest's Electrical Shop, standing next to the Market Place which is on the left of the picture, May 1986. Another of the family businesses which brought prosperity to the town, it continued to trade under this name until fairly recently when the Priest brothers retired and the firm was taken over by Chapman's of Old Hill. *(Ned Williams)*

The Bird family proudly display their fresh fruit and vegetables on the pavement outside the shop in High Street in the 1920s or '30s. Partially hidden behind the gas light at the top of the picture is a poster encouraging customers to join the Christmas Club. *(Malcolm Whitehouse)*

Another view of the fruit and vegetable shop in the High Street belonging to the Birds. *(Malcolm Whitehouse)*

The distinctive three-storey premises of the Eley brothers' butcher's shop in the High Street. The house and cart used for delivery is being led out of the entry separating the shop from the haberdashery business run by their sister. *(Philip Bannister)*

The Blackheath branch of Barclays Bank became a fully managed concern in 1897 in the Market Place, having previously been managed from Birmingham. It moved to 6 Halesowen Street in 1919. The building shown here opened in 1936 after the original premises had been enlarged and altered, and the bank remained there until it moved to its present location in Birmingham Road in 1982. The notice in the right-hand window welcomes new customers, stating that a new account can be opened for sums of £1 upwards. *(David Hickman)*

The furniture business of John T. Harris at 54/55 Birmingham Road, 1986. In addition to the showroom they also operated an upholstery business in Long Lane. Following redevelopment of the area they moved into the adapted schoolroom of Birmingham Road Methodist Church in 1987, where the business continues to be run by Stephen and Paul, two sons of Mr Harris. *(Ned Williams)*

Another of the town's established businesses belonged to J. Whittall, originally operating as a corn merchant, about halfway up High Street. By the time of this picture in 1984 the majority of their trade was in pet and garden supplies. *(Ned Williams)*

Situated in John Street, on the corner of Union Street, Thomas Howard Smith ran a house furnishing store. He was a prominent member of Birmingham Road Methodist Church, and was Superintendent of the Primary Department of the Sunday school for over fifty years. *(Author's Collection)*

The California in Halesowen Street stands almost at the junction with High Street, and has been there for a century or so. Next to it is a store which for many years was trading as a clothing supplier, initially owned by Mr Connop, of Halesowen, then passing to Mr Walker. At the time of this picture (early 1980s) it was a branch of Foster Brothers, but like so many other shops it has now become a building society. *(Ned Williams)*

Decimus Gaunt on the threshold of the Old Bush Revived in Powke Lane, a pub well patronised by the workers from nearby Lench's and the many miners who used to work in the various pits in the area. Decimus was one of the great characters in old Blackheath, keeping the pub for over half a century. One of the first coffins to be made for the respected Gaunt family firm of undertakers, which was started by Percival, the son of Decimus, was constructed in the loft of these premises. *(Margaret Guest)*

The original Britannia Inn in Halesowen Street in the early twentieth century. The landlady at the time of this picture was Charlotte Steventon Darby. This building was replaced in the late 1930s by the one which, after recent alterations, now trades as one of the J.D. Wetherspoon's chain. It still bears the same name. (*Malcolm Whitehouse*)

The Royal Oak was replaced by the current traffic island in the centre of town in about 1930. It had been the foremost coaching inn in the town for almost 300 years, serving initially as a toll house for the traffic between Halesowen and Oldbury. By the time of this picture we are into the modern motor coach era, but it was still an important stopping-off point. (*Fred Darby*)

Standing opposite the Rex Cinema (now Sainsburys) in Halesowen Street, this pub was known as the Little Beech to distinguish it from its namesake a little higher up the road. It is dustbin day at the time of the photograph in 1982. (*Terry Price*)

An unidentified group outside the same pub some years before, the landlord at the time being Ezra Homer. (*Malcolm Whitehouse*)

Another unidentified group waiting to board the magnificent old bus belonging to Halesowen Motor Transport, this time outside the County Hotel situated at the corner of Nimmings Road and Masters Lane, *c.* 1925. Because of the large wall-mounted clock the premises were known locally as the Clock, a name which eventually became their official title. (*Bob Grosvenor*)

For over a century the George & Dragon at the top of High Street became the name from which directions were given, being such a well-known landmark. Within the last few years it has changed its name to the Knight's Quest, but its appearance remains much the same. On the skyline at the right of the picture it is just possible to see the tower of St Giles's Parish Church, Rowley Regis. (*David Westwood*)

3

Schooldays

In 1980 Dr Barnardo's organised a Junior Mastermind competition, which was won by James Taylor, a pupil at Blackheath Junior & Infants School, Powke Lane. *(School Collection)*

From a production of *Aladdin in the Underground*, which took place in 1955 at Britannia Road School for Boys, we see the scene in the cave, where Aladdin (David Hancock) meets the Slave of the Ring (James Siviter). *(School Collection)*

The finale of the same production, in which the main characters were played by Anthony Heath, Robert Matthews, David Hancock, Stanley Aldridge, Gordon Potter, Handley Compton, James Siviter, Terence Wakeman, Robert Homer, Alan Insker and Edward Allen. Others taking part were John Bailey, David Barnsley, Alan Batham, Alan Bishop, Geoffrey Coleman, Eric Hipkiss, Keith Jones, John Kendick, Ronald Rhoden, Lawrence Rose, Charles Sheldon, Eric Weston, Clive Whittingham, Brian Willetts, Anthony Harris, John Hingley, Ronald Hodgetts, Raymond Parkes, Kenneth Turner, Gordon Willetts, Trevor Williams, David Worrall, Graham Aldridge, Barry Devonport, Wavell Hands, Geoffrey Matthews, John Mellor, Michael Plimmer, Jeffrey Caine, David Dingley, Joseph Edwards, Arthur Harris, Jack Head, Alan Jones, Brian Marshall, David Osborne, James Taylor, Ralph Tromans, Brian Webster and Brian Wellings. *(School Collection)*

A class at Holt Road Junior School in 1950 showing the headmaster Mr Blackford and form teacher Mrs Pembridge. The pupils include Barry Smith, Terry Jones, Phillip Johnson, Michael Stone, Geoffrey Gadd, David Detheridge, Colin James, Jeffrey Pugh, Rex Hill, Robert Moore, Jeffrey Griffin, John Dyas, Paul Harper, Jennifer Sankey, Yvonne Parkes, Judith Cowley, Margaret Adams, Judith Bagley, Pat Hovells, Muriel Green, Terry Hickman, Michael Hollies, Pauline Farmer, Wendy Bernard, Enid Raybould, Brenda Harrold, Yvonne Thompson, Josie Nicklin, Vaire James, Judy Lappage, Julia Hughes, Nadine Lewis and Carol Hill. *(Enid Bissell)*

The previous year, 1949, this time in the Holt Road Infants School. Pupils include Robert Moore, Jeffrey Hinton, Michael Holbee, Terry Jones, Paul Harper, John Dyas, Colin James, Barry Smith, Michael Stone, Terry Hickman, Rex Hill, Jeffrey Griffin. Raymond Merris, Geoffrey Gadd, Alan Law, Yvonne Parkes, Judith Bagley, Mary Adams, Muriel Green, Jennifer Sankey, Margaret Hill, Janet Bell, Pauline Farmer, Wendy Wrigley, David Detheridge, Peter Tibbetts. Yvonne Thompson, Judith Windsor, Margaret Doyle, Pat Willetts, Wendy Bennett, Enid Raybould, Carol Hill, Judy Lappage, Vaire James, Dawn Mole, Eileen Basterfield, ? Holland, Paul James, Alan Whitehouse, Jeffrey Howarth, Alan Parkes and Phillip Johnson. *(Enid Bissell)*

The football team of 1947 from Beeches Road School. The teacher is Mr Nock. Back row, left to right: Barry Brazier, David Levett, Keith Plunkett, Gordon Parsons, David Wright, Tony Goddard, Jimmy Ruston. Front row: ? Davies, Ray Darby, Geoff Taylor, Alan Bateman, John Copson. *(Gordon Parsons)*

Pupils from Hill and Cakemore School are dressed up representing various Commonwealth countries to celebrate Empire Day 1929. *(Author's Collection)*

The staff at Britannia Road School, 1956. Back row, left to right: W. Gee, B.J. Christopher, F.N. Stirrup, J.H. Walton, C.E.S. Harris, D. Matthews, S.E. Mugglestone, K. Thomas. Middle row: J. Sidaway, T.A. Porter, N.M. Neale, H. Wyle, W.J. Haine, C.W. Gains, C. Woodward, A. Parsons, W. Brittain. Front row: R. Hackett, A. Johnson, F.E. Sidaway, G.A. Willetts (headmaster), Mrs E. Matthews (school secretary), C. Richards, A.M. Green. *(School Collection)*

The Britannia Road School Swimming Gala winners and runners-up, 1970. Back row, left to right: Mr J. Walton, S. Fox, J. Botfield, S. Singh, R. Wimbush, S. Bale, H. Sheppard, Mr Thomas. Middle row: K. Payne, C. King, S. Siviter, G. Smith, T. Ashman, P. Haynes, P. Westwood, T. Nock, J. Hill, A. Epstein, D. Elliott. Front row: M. Davies, G. Davies, D. Smart, G. Saint, Mr D. Greville (headmaster), S. Wattley, S. Holland, J. Woodward, T. Woodall. *(School Collection)*

The Powke Lane Football Team pose in the school playground, 1955/6. Back row, left to right: -?-, Kenneth Court, David Williams, Christopher Tranter, Terry Gibbons, Graham James, Godfrey Crompton, John Turbill, -?-. Front row: Stuart Siviter, Michael Guise, Roger Sturman (captain), -?-, David Powell. The headmaster Mr Ray Richards is in the centre of the three teachers. *(School Collection)*

Rowley Regis Secondary Boys' School held their annual prize distribution on 19 July 1956. Here we see Mr G.T. Lloyd MA, Headmaster, Rowley Regis Grammar School (extreme right), presenting the Hobbs Cup House Trophy to Alfred Evans, the Captain, and Mr D. Matthews, the Housemaster, of the Normans House. The school's headmaster, Mr G. A. Willetts, is in attendance. *(School Collection)*

A class of girls from Hill and Cakemore Girls' School, 1958. Their identities are not known. (*Margaret Patrick*)

Some of the teaching staff from Beeches Road School in the early twentieth century. The picture is taken near the floral border in the garden of the caretaker's house, with the cottages in Beeches Road in the background, looking in the general direction of Cocksheds Lane. (*Joseph Jones*)

The boys of Britannia Road School had many extra-curricular activities from which to choose. Here we have a group belonging to the Model Railway Club, with teacher Gil Barnett in the centre of the track layout, and Ivan Southall at the extreme right. *(Ivan Southall)*

Another class from Holt Road Primary School in 1949. Back row, left to right: -?-, David Adams, Fred Doody, Roger Griffiths, Grandy Law, Alan Pearson, John Tromans, -?-, Barry Faulkener, Tony Downing. Third row: Ray Ruston, Carol Young, Sally Smith, Iris Parkes, Margaret Phipps, Ann Preece, Margaret Hill, Margaret Perks, Hilda Pearson, Norma Garvey, Colin Parkes. Second row: John Costello, Mary Whitehouse, Marjorie Bate, Keith Neale, Eileen Clift, Jean Whittall, Rhoda Bennett, Pamela Sankey, Lilian Thompson, Lorna Bytheway. Front row: Ray Brookes, John Mills, Michael Law, John Crompton, John Howard, Ray Hancox. The headmaster, W.W. Blackford, is on the left. *(Ray Ruston)*

Children from Holt Road Infants School are all dressed up for a display of physical education at a fete held on the British Thompson Houston (BTH) playing fields, 6 July 1928. (*Author's Collection*)

At the same event it is the turn of the Church of England Infants School, in Long Lane, to present a programme of country dances in costume. (*Author's Collection*)

Because of the large number of pupils Beeches Road Junior School had to have some of their lessons in the schoolroom of Birmingham Road Methodist Church. Here we see one of the classes in 1953. Back row, left to right: Rita Hadley, -?-, Margaret Mathews, John Homer, Terry Masterson, Pauline Detheridge, John Walters, Kay Hadley, -?-, David Payne, Dave Lenton, Stuart Hayes. Middle row: Barbara Bootton, Phil Harris, Judith Williams, David Hadley, -?-, -?-, -?-, -?-, Anthony B. Smith, Ann Brain, Jill Bagley, Robert Bannister, Mr Poole (class teacher). Front row: Derek Northall, Anthony P. Smith, Mack Hadley, -?-, Mick Bowater, Celia Beddows, Pauline Sidaway, -?-, Christine Harris, Alan Keightley, Tony Hingley, -?-, Diane Bloor. Seated on mats: Martin Hemmings, -?-, Raymond Goode, Terry Bowater, ? Lovall, John Johnson. (*Michael Bowater*)

A year later (1954) many of the same pupils are now in Class IIIA. Back row, left to right: -?-, Jill Bagley, Martin Hemmings, David Hadley, Ann Brain, Judith Williams, -?-, -?-, Pauline Detheridge, Margaret Mathews, Barbara Bootton, -?-, Anthony B. Smith. Middle row: -?-, Brian Harris, Terry Bowater, Stuart Hayes, -?-, Trevor Parkes, Philip Harris, Robert Bannister, Ray Goode, John Homer, John Johnson, Kay Hadley. Front row: Dave Lenton, -?-, Mack Hadley, Derek Northall, Alan Keightley, Tony Hingley, Miss Downing (class teacher), Christine Harris, Celia Beddows, Rita Hadley, Pauline Sidaway, Diane Bloor, Mick Bowater. Seated on floor: -?-, Anthony P. Smith. (*Michael Bowater*)

Some of the children from Causeway Green Infants School presented the play entitled *How to be Healthy, Wealthy and Wise* at the gala on 6 July 1928 at the BTH playing fields, as part of the Infant Welfare Week for that year. *(Author's Collection)*

Britannia High School, 1990. The school opened on 2 July 1932 as the principal school for boys in Rowley Regis, with Mr J.L. Johnson as headmaster. It was well known for the many sporting activities some of which are illustrated in this book, with its own sports field and swimming baths. Owing to reorganisation the school closed in 2004 and was demolished and replaced by new premises to accommodate the scholars from Powke Lane Junior and Infants School. *(School Collection)*

An aerial view of the area at the top of High Street, with Powke Lane School in the centre, mid-1970s. The crossroads shows Holly Road, High Street, Ross and Powke Lane, and the old houses and shops in High Street, opposite the premises of John Tooth can be seen, before being cleared to make way for the Elizabeth Prout Gardens complex. In the foreground is part of the factory premises of T.W. Lench Ltd. In recent years almost the whole of the area to the right of Ross and Holly Road have been subject to large housing developments *(Author's Collection)*

Local schools were encouraged to compete against each other for the Road Safety Shield presented by Joseph Billingham, a local industrialist, which was won in 1963 by the girls from Siviters Lane. Long-serving headmistress Mrs M. Westwood BA is second from the left. *(Maud Shaw)*

Class III of the British National School, *c.* 1890. This was one of the first schools in the district, and ultimately became Powke Lane Junior and Infants School. *(Iris Lee)*

The championship chess team from Blackheath Junior School, 1989. Back row, left to right: Mark Lees, Chris Bills, Ian Evans, Philip Baker, Joseph Mason, Keith Lees. Seated: James Whittington, Angela Jeffs, -?-. *(School Collection)*

The school band from Beeches Road Junior School, mid-1950s, with Roger Barker second from the right on the back row. *(Doris Barker)*

A party of over 300 girls, staff and parents from Siviters Lane School visited London, including a tour of the House of Commons, on 27 June 1952. Here we see some of them relaxing on the terrace. *(Maud Shaw)*

As part of the centenary celebrations of Powke Lane School, on Monday 29 October 1979, Class 2D (3rd year) are in the playground in Victorian dress, as they prepare to go on a trip to the Severn Valley Railway. Lucy Witherington is shown dropping a curtsy for the camera. *(School Collection)*

The Blackheath Junior (Powke Lane) Football Team of 1948–9. The teachers on the back row are Mr Beasley, Mr Richards (headmaster) and Mr Willetts. Second row: A. Baker, Johnny Bowater, Colin Bagley, C. Mason, Ivan Southall, Arthur South. Front row: D. Humphries, Colin Millinchip, Wesley Potter (captain), Derek Hale, J. Simpson. *(School Collection)*

The girls of Siviters Lane School present the first of their annual Christmas plays, *The Singing Shepherd* by Phyllis Stone, in 1949. The principal part of Nathan was taken by Doreen Price, who is seated at the front right. *(Maud Shaw)*

The premises of St Paul's Church of England School in Long Lane are empty and await demolition to make way for the sheltered housing complex aptly named St Paul's Court, *c.* 1970. *(Author's Collection)*

A class at Beeches Road Junior School, 1928–9. Pupils include K. Downing, ? Guest, N. Lightfoot, E. Hadley and M. Bussey. *(Leslie Bird)*

The pupils of Powke Lane Junior School put on a dancing display in the school playground for parents and friends, to mark the Festival of Britain in 1951. *(School Collection)*

More pupils from Powke Lane School, this time in 1977, when they held a sponsored spell in order to raise funds for the school reference library. (*School Collection*)

4

Church & Chapel Life

In the early 1970s the Blackheath Methodist Circuit Education and Youth Committee held an Annual Eisteddfod for the young and not so young to showcase their artistic talents. The overall best performance by an individual church was awarded the Annual Shield, and in 1973 it was won by Heath Street. Here we see, left to right, Mrs Hyde, the Revd John Hope, Panima Patel, Joe Hewitt, Carole Pocknell and the Revd Robert B. Hyde (Superintendent Minister). *(Eric Parkes)*

The Revd J. Clifford Adams was part of a family of preachers who initially belonged to the Heath Street Methodist Church. His father, Will Adams, and brother, Arthur, were local preachers, but Clifford became an ordained minister and held appointments in many parts of the country, including a spell on the staff of Luton Industrial College. He was a devoted supporter of West Bromwich Albion, travelling to see many matches even in his more senior years. He died in 2005. *(Author's Collection)*

Members of Malt Mill Lane Methodist Church assemble with their banner in readiness to join the Annual Sunday School Procession in the mid-1920s. *(Joyce Bennett)*

Some members of the Heath Street Methodist Women's Own Class on a day's outing in the mid-1950s are seen at the Nags Head where they had stopped for refreshments. The location is not known. Among those present are Mary Goode, Dora Blakeway, Phyllis Basterfield, Mrs Rebecca Goode, Mrs Andrews, Lily and Betty Asson, Mrs Ingram, Mrs Willetts, Mrs Blakeway, Florrie Asson, Ethel Harvey, Hilda Whorton, Mrs Mary Parkes, Mrs Sarah Evans. *(Eric Parkes)*

Some of the menfolk belonging to the Bethel Fellowship in Vicarage Road, including Frank Webster and George Hackett, are seen during the rebuilding of the church, which opened in May 1967. *(Christine Lees)*

An outing from Birmingham Road Methodist Church, 1950s. The group includes Les and Alice Baker, Bert and Mrs Harris and their daughter Maureen, Fred and Edie Adams, Albert and Mrs Willetts and Mrs Hussey. *(James Adams)*

Another group of Blackheath Methodist people on holiday in the early 1960s, perhaps at Blackpool. Included are Edna Wootton, May Jones, Polly Westwood, Emily Adams, Mrs Payne, Edith Nock, Walter Wootton, Olive Wootton, Fred Sawyer, Ernest Parkes, Mrs Hussey, Fred Honeysett, Barbara Honeysett, John Hussey, Estella Hancox. (*Barbara Honeysett*)

Birmingham Road Methodist Church is clearly visible through the rubble in this view taken from Oldbury Road during clearance of the area in 1976. (*Author's Collection*)

Representatives attending the Synod of the Birmingham District of the Methodist Church are caught by the camera outside the High Street Methodist Church, mid-1920s. *(Author's Collection)*

The new Sunday School buildings of Birmingham Road Methodist Church were opened on Thursday 16 February 1933 at a service conducted by the Revd George Froggatt. Plans for the building had commenced in 1926 under the leadership of the Revd Thomas Jukes. Here we see Mr Samuel James Parkes officially opening the doors for the first time. (*Barbara Honeysett*)

Margaret Mole and her sister Dulcie Green hand over the ceremonial key used by their father Samuel James Parkes to open Birmingham Road Sunday School to Fred Ingram, long-term Property Secretary and Sunday School worker. This was done at a concert to mark the closure of the building as a Sunday School in September 1985, before its sale for use as a showroom for John T. Harris's furniture store. (*Anthony Page*)

It is believed that this picturesque cottage in Yew Tree Lane was where the first members of the Methodist New Connexion held their earliest meetings in 1840, before renting rooms in Siviters Lane and then moving to found what was to become Birmingham Road Methodist Church. The photograph dates from the early 1920s. *(Author's Collection)*

A garden party was held in 1973, in the grounds of Olive House, Halesowen Street, on behalf of Birmingham Road Methodist Church. Left to right are the Revd George and Mrs Lilian Price (Superintendent Minister and his wife), Fred and Emily Ingram (hosts) and the Revd George and Mrs Vera Roberts (Minister of High Street Church and his wife). *(Anthony Page)*

Arthur Hall (Sunday School Secretary and Trustee), Rebecca Goode (the oldest member and President of the Women's Own Class for over forty years) and Eric Parkes (Organist and Trustee), are pictured at the opening of the new Heath Street Independent Methodist Church, which took place in 1976. *(Eric Parkes)*

Following the deprivations of the Second World War the folk of Blackheath took every possible opportunity to go on trips to the countryside or the sea, and every year the choir members of Birmingham Road Methodist Church organised such outings. In the upper picture, from about 1963, Janet Mole and Ann Cutler are enjoying a moment of relaxation, and the three men in a boat in the lower picture are Frank Green (organist), the Revd Charles T. Santry (minister) and Horace Powell (deputy organist) at Windermere in the Lake District in 1965. *(Anthony Page)*

Three young ladies from the Bethel Sunday School, Vicarage Road, are all dressed up for the Sunday School Anniversary in 1957. They are, from left to right, Cynthia Merchill, Janet Crump and Christine Webster. (*Christine Lees*)

Most of the Sunday Schools in the Blackheath Area competed in the Annual Scripture Examination and the ones with the highest average were awarded the Challenge Shield by the local Sunday School Union. The winners in 1956 were the Bethel, Vicarage Road, and here we see, from left to right, Molly Feraby, Christine Webster, Janet Poynter, Cynthia Merchill, Pearl Lee, Leonard Harris, -?-, Doreen ?, George Hackett, June Ashmore, Mr Alfred Mole, Mrs Ivy Webster, Veronica Lee, Chris Lloyd, Paul Hackett, Janet Crump. (*Christine Lees*)

After the renovations to Birmingham Road Methodist Church in 1986 the Sunday School scholars were presented with commemorative mugs, and among those in this picture are Timothy and Vicky Andrews, Timothy and Christopher Page, John and Simon Gardner, Rachel and John Chambers, Tanya and Tina Horley, Rebecca Rainey, Teresa Plant, Melanie Smith, Rachel Wood, Jane Bowater, with teachers Jenny Andrews, Margaret Wooldridge, Fred Ingram, Gwen Davies and the Minister, the Revd Colin Gardner. *(Anthony Page)*

Scholars from Beeches Road Sunday School are seen at the annual Sunday School Anniversary, 1955. Back row, left to right: -?-, Diane Cole, Sheila Dudley, Margaret Smith, the Revd Caddy, Sheila Gardner, Diane Richards, Sheila Downing, Mary Webster. Third row: Colin Parkes, Sandra Ravenscroft, Margaret Cartwright, -?-, Dilys Parkes, Joyce Meakin, Joan Gardner, Sandra Pearce, Lorna Dallow, -?-. Second row: Trevor Parkes, Robert Downing, Christine Edwards, -?-, Glynis Darby, Christine Parkes, June Sherwood, Yvonne Woodhall, -?-, -?-. Front row: -?-, Margaret Parkes, Lynette? Pearce, -?-, Flora Meakin, -?-, -?-, Sheila Woodhall, Anne Marie Woodhall, Madge Parkes, David? Meakin.*(Arnold Tromans)*

This photograph was taken in 1958 to celebrate the fiftieth anniversary of the opening of the new building of Long Lane Methodist Church. *(Rita Box)*

The choir and members of the congregation of Long Lane Methodist Church prepare to go on the choir outing in 1949. Note the building behind them attached to the house on the right is the Council Infant Welfare Centre, which was open on Wednesday and Thursday afternoons. *(Rita Box)*

The original Whiteheath Methodist Church opened in 1842 and was situated in Birchfield Lane, on the right-hand side going towards Oldbury. The building was altered in 1873 to the one shown here, the exterior (above) and the interior. Although physically situated in Oldbury it was part of the Blackheath (Birmingham Road) Circuit. The photographs date from the mid-1940s. *(Author's Collection)*

Pictured in about 1952, this choir was founded by Mr Cyril Parsons (the back of whose head is visible at the front), and performed under the name of Gorsty Hill and District Choir. Performing mainly at Gorsty Hill Methodist Church, they also gave concerts at other local churches, chapels and cinemas, even cutting a 78rpm record which was sold locally. *(Doreen Tolley)*

Fifty years later a reunion was held for surviving members, and they sang some of their old favourites. Among those pictured are Joyce Brazier, Myrtle Smith, Val Pearson, Christine Allport, Ann Green, Pat Priest, Irene Guest, Elsie Nock, Freda Burrows, Sheila Kite, Ann Spencer, Pearl Smith, Doreen Tolley, Margaret Baxter, with Paul Priest and Maurice Smith at the back. *(Doreen Tolley)*

The Revd John T. Gray opens the new Whiteheath Methodist Church in June 1956, watched over by the Revd W. Russell Shearer MA (Chairman of the Birmingham District of the Methodist Church) and George Round (trustee of the church). On the extreme left is Mr Stanley Griffiths, the architect responsible for the design. *(Author's Collection)*

The strikingly modern interior of the new building is quite significantly different from its predecessor (page 75). *(Author's Collection)*

The Revd John T. Gray was also involved in the building of the Sunday School extension for another of the churches on the Blackheath Circuit, Malt Mill Lane, and here he is seen at the stone-laying ceremony in October 1953. *(Author's Collection)*

Scholars from the Sunday School at Malt Mill Lane enjoy their outing to Habberley Valley, near Kidderminster, summer 1957. *(Joyce Bennett)*

Beeches Road Sunday School Anniversary, 1953. Back row, left to right: Terry Jones, Cynthia Hill, Brenda Booth, Sheila Gardner, Margaret Edwards, Diane Richards, Jean Millinchip, Doreen Parkes, John Harris. Third row: -?-, Margaret Smith, Gillian Bagley, -?-, Joyce Meakin, -?-, Sheila Dudley, Maureen Carter, Colin Parkes. Second row: Godfrey Crumpton, Diane Cole, -?-, Sheila Downing, -?-, Margaret Cartwright, Lorna Dallow, Joan Gardner, Sandra Pearce, -?-. Front row: Trevor Parkes, -?-, Christine Parkes, June Sherwood, -?-, Flora Meakin, Yvonne Woodall, Doris Shaw, -?-, -?-. *(Len Parkes)*

The large audience at a concert held to mark the sale of the Sunday School buildings at Birmingham Road Methodist Church, September 1985. Among those visible on the upper picture are Rachel Wood, Paula Smith, Keith and Gwen Davies, Fred Ingram, Margaret Wooldridge, Margaret Mole, Elsie Ovenstone, Horace and Dulcie Green, Arthur and Joyce Wood, Francis Jarvis, Janet Page, Jim and Enid Parry, Norman and Irene Siviter. In the lower picture are Tim and Chris Page, Robert Masterson, Melanie Smith, Amanda Faulkner, Joe Hewitt, John Chambers, John Johnson, Fred and Barbara Honeysett, Mrs Bagley, Nina Thomas, Ann Harris, Polly Fletcher, Christine Chambers, Terry and Margaret Martin, Brian and Dora Bubb, Geoff, Marlene and Mark Wootton, Les and Mary Woodall. *(Anthony Page)*

'The tin chapel', the schoolroom of the Congregational Church in Green Lane, July 1930. One of the prototype flat-pack constructions, this type of building was found up and down the country, but few remain today. At the time of the picture it was used in the week as the Hill and Cakemore Infant Welfare Clinic, and today is a day centre for Age Concern. *(Author's Collection)*

Members of Cocksheds Methodist Church with their banner, 1920s. The back row includes, left to right: A. Jackson, W. Pearson, S. White, the Revd P. Shaw, D. Goode, E. Smith, B. Law. Front row: N. Adams, D. Potter, E. Perks, L. Clift, E. Harris, L. Whittall, M. Greaves, L. Lowe, C. Love. *(Alan Bennett)*

A group of members from the Blackheath Congregational Church in the 1920s, the only three named being Tom Kite (fourth from left), Ernest Fearnley (centre of picture) and George Gregory. *(Ivan Williams)*

The annual Whit Monday procession and treat pauses on the car park of the George & Dragon in High Street for a short open-air service, mid-1960s. *(Anthony Page)*

The Birmingham Road Methodist Sunday School banner with party outside the church in Causeway, 1930s. Among those present are Fred Adams, Ben Parkes and Arthur Page. *(James Adams)*

The Birmingham Road Methodist Youth Club production of *Rajah of Rajahpore*, 1946. Standing, left to right: Harold Yates, Jean Edwards, Arthur Parkes, Barbara Dunn, John Green, Sydney Churchill, Phillip Levett, Fred Honeysett. Seated: Pearl Allen, Olive Burchell, Barbara Poole, Vera Grant. *(Barbara Honeysett)*

The Revd David Hobson (Circuit Minister) is seen judging the Senior Fancy Dress Competition at the Circuit Garden Party held in the grounds of Hurst Green Church in July 1984. Among the competitors are Christopher Page, Jonathan Gardner and Joanne Church. *(Anthony Page)*

Two pictures taken at the stone-laying ceremony for the new Sunday School building at Birmingham Road Methodist Church, 1932. In the upper photograph (*Ernest Honeysett*) the assembled crowd watches while the commemorative foundation stones are laid, and this was followed by an open air tea party, obviously enjoyed by the young people decked out in their Sunday best. (*Barbara Honeysett*)

The Revd George Kenneth Morgan Green was appointed Vicar of St Paul's Church, Blackheath, on 2 December 1906 and was inducted into his post by Canon Hill on 2 February 1907. He served until September 1912, when he became Vicar of Malvern Wells and was replaced by the Revd D.J. Scurry Jones. *(Author's Collection)*

The Revd W.J. Harries, who was minister at the Blackheath Congregational Church between November 1906 and November 1918. *(Ivan Williams)*

The Sunday School scholars and staff of Heath Street Methodist Church pose outside the old Ebenezer Chapel in 1973. Included are Clive Temple, Cissie Hall, Martin Hingley, Tom Hadley, Kevin Smith, Ted Baker, Steven Burgoyne, Philip Blakeway, Beverley King, May Dunn, Ivy Hall, Arthur Hall, Elaine Adams and Emma Hadley. *(Eric Parkes)*

5

Work & Leisure

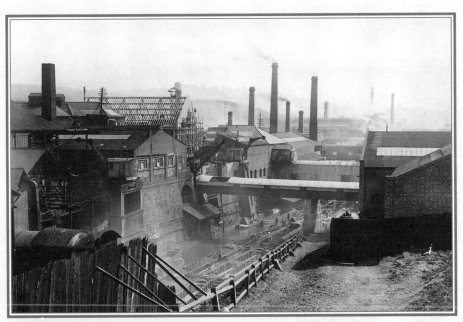

A postcard view of the Coombs Wood Steelworks, probably taken in the 1930s when it was trading as Stewarts & Lloyds before becoming part of British Steel. The canal, with a large number of narrowboats carrying coal to the works, runs diagonally through the picture. In recent years the whole complex has been flattened and is now trading as a varied factory estate, including the local post office sorting complex. (*Betty Johnson*)

The workforce is assembled at the BTH works to listen to an address, although the occasion is not known. *(Charles Morgan)*

Taking a break from their duties, the typing office staff of Stewarts & Lloyds is seen in this line-up from 1949. The photograph was taken beside the General Office. Left to right: Dorothy Whitehouse, Cynthia Lewis, Betty Holland, Maisie Crockett, Connie Priest, Jean Chatwin, Eric Goode, Grace Thompson, Gladys Whittle, Iris Harris, Freda Darby, Barbara Towers, Joyce Holden and Mabel Lear. *(Betty Johnson)*

Situated in Cakemore Road was the Shell UK Terminal, and here are the road vehicle loading bays as they were in the late 1970s. The depot closed for business in April 1985. *(Enid Bissell)*

A regular sight for travellers from Blackheath to Langley was this BTH shunting engine, as it moved from the works towards the main railway line on other side of Cakemore Road. The photograph was taken in the mid-1980s. *(CHAS)*

Some of the workers at Zachariah Clay's rivet-making factory. The lad holding the samples at the front is his younger son Zachariah Matthews (Matt). Zachariah Senior was the son-in-law of Daniel Matthews, who was a preacher belonging to Providence Baptist Chapel, Bell End. This picture dates from between 1885 and 1890. *(Margaret Carter)*

Within the grounds of Stewarts & Lloyds steelworks stood the Coombs Wood Institute. The chief feature of this fine building, erected by the firm in 1913 for the benefit of Tube Works employees, was a large hall with an ample stage, which was used as a dining room by day and as a place of entertainment in the evening. Many fine performances were given in the hall, which at the time was one of the largest in Midlands, including those by an amateur operatic company and a male voice choir, each made up of Coombs Wood employees. *(David Hickman)*

A group of Blackheath Building workers on a day off from work, including Ernest Wyle, roofer and tiler (in trilby sitting in the centre), Will Parkes, builder (extreme left), G. Dingley and Dick Taylor (standing at the rear right) who used to work for Ernest Wyle, and ? Parkes, who was an electrician. *(Frank Wyle)*

Stewarts & Lloyds were pioneers in the manufacture of seamless steel pipe work, using electric welding, which they developed in the 1920s. *(Author's Collection)*

The Stewarts & Lloyds Male Voice Choir, who were well known not only in the immediate locality but across the Midlands, performing in places as distant as Leamington Spa. The photograph was taken in about 1950. *(Harry Bateman)*

The chorus line from the BTH Operatic Society performance of *The Gondoliers. (Charles Morgan)*

Employees of Stewarts & Lloyds in full evening dress outside the Institute make up the works concert orchestra. *(David Hickman)*

Stewarts & Lloyds Operatic Group presented a performance of *The Vagabond King* in 1928, which was held in the works canteen and attracted audiences in excess of 200 people. In the upper photograph we see Harry and Frances Bateman, and in the lower one there are more members of the cast. *(Harry Bateman)*

Here we see railcars being shunted into the storage bays at the Shell Terminal in Cakemore Road, 1983. *(Enid Bissell)*

A full range of sporting activities was offered to the workforce at Stewarts & Lloyds, so in addition to the more usual football and cricket teams they also ran a rugby team, pictured here outside the pavilion in Gorsty Hill in 1934. *(Elsie Scarrott)*

In order to give their employees a period of time in the open air, and to help restore the agricultural labour force after the Second World War, the Stewarts & Lloyds Group allowed people from all their factories to spend a week pea picking. Among those pictured from the Coombs Wood factory are (back

row) Des Barlow, (middle row) Margery Millward, Dorothy Whitehouse, Betty Holland, Doreen Parsons, Jean Downing, Betty Brittain, (front row) Vera Shufflebotham, Doris Harrison. *(Betty Johnson)*

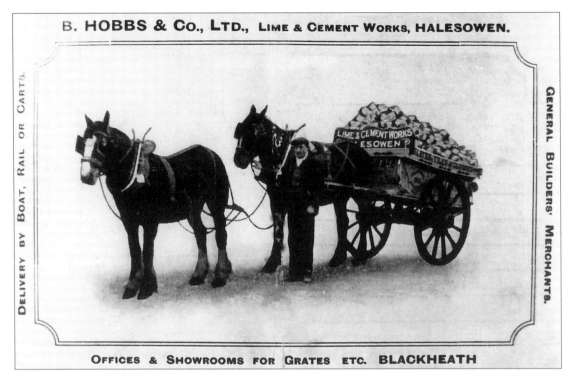

Ben Hobbs, the first Charter Mayor of Rowley Regis, was a local industrialist who specialised in making bricks and running a builders merchants, but became famous for the supply of fire-grates, which were sold all over the wider West Midlands area. Here we have a 1930s postcard advertising some of his lines of business. *(Maisie Hayman)*

In common with most factories, BTH ran their own Fire Brigade, and here they are seen on their annual camp in the mid-1920s. The camp was held in conjunction with other branches of the company from around the country. *(Doreen Sawyer)*

BTH organised an Annual Gala for their employees and members of the general public, which was held on the sports ground in Cakemore Road. This tug-of-war demonstrates plenty of enthusiasm. It took place sometime in the 1960s. *(Charles Morgan)*

During one of the 'Special Dances' which were held in the Works Concert Hall at BTH, which could accommodate up to 400 people, these are some of the entrants to the annual Glamorous Grannies Contest of 1967. Les While is in the centre. Doris Swain is on the extreme left and Doris Flavell next to her. *(Les While)*

The football team of St James's Mission, a daughter church of St Paul's which was situated in Waterfall Lane, early twentieth century. *(Author's Collection)*

Mrs Martha Newman of Carlyle Road is pictured with two of her friends during the annual hop-picking holiday, shortly after the Second World War. *(Morris Newman)*

Two staff members of the Custard Powder Factory, situated in Cardale Street, are seen with their delivery van with its advertising slogan of 'Double Yolk' Custard Powder, 1920s. The firm was part of the business of Price's Manufacturing Chemists, operating retail establishments around the town, including a shop in the High Street. *(Black Country Bugle)*

One of the trams which ran between Blackheath and Cradley Heath, *c.* 1900. The driver is Wilf Body from Cinder Bank, Netherton, and the conductor Jack Roe. Local adverts include Walker's Clothiers & Outfitters of Blackheath and Cradley Heath, and W. Darby, the People's Cash Draper, of Blackheath. *(Philip Body)*

The horse-drawn hearse belonging to the undertaking firm of Hadley Brothers is about to set off from their base in Vicarage Road, with Charles Hadley at the reins. *(Stephen Downing)*

Members of the Willetts family are seen outside the garage belonging to Orchard Confectionery in Holly Road, 1920s. *(Malcolm Whitehouse)*

6

People

Amy Brettle spent most of her life in the St John Ambulance Brigade,
and was awarded one of the highest honours available within the organisation.
For a large part of that time she was responsible for the training of nursing
cadets, and she is pictured here on the right with a group
of her young charges. *(Amy Bussey)*

The Hill and Cakemore Infant Welfare Committee of 1929 consisted of Mrs C. Moore (Hon. Sec.), Mrs Lowe, Mrs Willetts, Mrs Parkes, Mrs Adams and Mrs Cooper, who are seen here with Dr Bulmer and Nurse O'Grady outside the centre in Green Lane. *(Author's Collection)*

Members of the Royal British Legion Club, whose headquarters are in Powke Lane, are seen here with their families at a Christmas party, 1950s. *(May Botfield)*

Honeysett's Bakery was situated on Shell Corner at the junction of Long Lane with Belgrave Road, and here we see Joe Dudley and Frank Honeysett in the yard with their horse-drawn delivery cart, mid-1920s. *(Ernest Honeysett)*

Joseph Mallin and his family are seen in the 1930s outside the original Pear Tree Inn in Mincing Lane, where he was landlord for a considerable time. This picturesque building was later replaced by a modern one, but in the 1990s made way for housing developments. (*Author's Collection*)

Harry William Grosvenor is pictured at home in New John Street in the latest model pedal car. Someone has pencilled in a cigar and inscribed the picture 'Winston Churchill' because of the boy's similarity in appearance to the great man. (*Bob Grosvenor*)

Mr Nelson and Mrs Gail Moore and family in their pony and trap, with a thatched cottage in Causeway in the background. This cottage is believed to have been built in the early nineteenth century and remained until about 1920 when the council houses were put up. Nelson Moore and William E. Moore were well known for their fresh fish shop in High Street. They had three children, William, Nelson and May. *(Author's Collection)*

Members of the 1st Rowley Scout Troop are seen in Britannia Park attending the local carnival, with the houses of Mackmillan Road in the background. They had just taken part in a tug-of-war competition. Back row, left to right: Geoff Grant, Glanfor Owens, -?-, George Whittall, -?- , Les ?, Robert Overfield. Front row: -?-, Mr Biggs, Tony Homer, Les Crump, Ron Wood. *(Glanfor Owens)*

Fanny Aston outside the family shop which was opposite the main entrance to Stewarts & Lloyds, Coombs Wood Works, and so did a roaring trade with the workers on their way to and from work, 1920s. (*Sue Pearson*)

A group of infant welfare officials outside the Congregational Church in Long Lane, pictured before a public meeting to emphasise the importance of correct child rearing practices to the nation, 1 July 1928. Left to right, standing: Mrs Willetts, Mrs Rock, Dr Wyndham Parker (County Medical Officer for Worcestershire), Nurse Cameron, Mrs Lowe. Seated: Dr E.N. Paterson (Medical Officer for Halesowen Infant Welfare) and Miss Morson (Superintendent of Health Visitors for Malvern). *(Author's Collection)*

This group of children is at a wedding party outside the British Restaurant in Birmingham Road, mid-1940s. The photograph includes Paul Harris, Catherine Parsons, Gweneth Fisher, Michael Hadley, Stephen Harris, Victoria Willetts, Lynn Willetts, David Hadley, Neil Harris and John Willetts. *(Gwen Davies)*

Four Gaunt brothers, sons of Decimus, in a car belonging to their uncle Richard, who was Mayor of Stockton-on-Tees, *c.* 1920. He had left the Black Country, and in the words of the family 'had gone up in the world, and used to swank a lot'. The brothers are William, Percy (later to become the undertaker), Howard and Lawrence. *(Peter Gaunt)*

The Hobbs family pictured at the back of their home, Regis House, Causeway, late 1920s. They are Dorothy, Eleanor, Elizabeth, Enoch, Benjamin, Victor, Mary and Emily. *(Robert Hobbs)*

Mr and Mrs Holmes are pictured in Britannia Park with their infant son, Raymond, early 1930s. Bill was a well-known character in Blackheath, as he ran a newsagent's shop in Birmingham Road, and also had a pitch on Blackheath station to sell to the travellers. He was seldom seen without a cigarette in his hand. On his death the business was continued by his widow and daughter. *(Ray Holmes)*

The Taylor family, in a photograph possibly taken in West Street, early 1900s. *(David Taylor)*

Because of the poverty of the area many children were encouraged to scavenge among the pit mounds for any loose coal that might be available, and it is believed that this group was to be found on the Station Colliery in about 1910. The group includes Fred Parkes behind the girl in the centre holding a hammer. *(Black Country Bugle)*

A group of mothers and babies outside the Kings Theatre in Long Lane, July 1929. They had been invited along by Mr Cooper, the proprietor, for a free show, not of the latest blockbuster release from Hollywood, but of government educational films about child-rearing practices. (*Author's Collection*)

Ladies from the Darby & Joan club, run by Gladys Gaunt, who is standing just to the right of coach in the white hat and coat, all ready for a day trip organised by Florrie Dunn, the well-known Blackheath coach owner. They are waiting outside the George & Dragon in High Street; Howell's carpet shop can be seen in the background, by the entrance to Shepherd's Fold. The picture dates from the late 1960s. (*Leslie Bird*)

Tommy Smart was born in Blackheath, and lived for most of his life in Birmingham Road. He became a professional footballer with Aston Villa, for whom he played from 1919 to 1933. Tommy won nine England caps. Widely regarded as one of the greatest full-backs in the history of the club, he was a formidable opponent. *(Paul Jameson)*

A group of Blackheath businessmen in Ben Hobbs's garden in Causeway. Recognisable are Ben Hobbs (seated to the left of the fountain) and Percival Gaunt (standing to the right of the fountain), with Sergeant Salt, landlord of the George & Dragon, to his right. *(Peter Gaunt)*

The wedding of Zachariah Matthews (Matt) Clay and Annie Sturman, September 1900, thought to be taken in front of old thatched cottages at the top of Causeway. Also in the picture are Will Sturman, Matilda Sturman, Flora (Florrie) Sturman, Fred Tromans (who married Flora in 1902), Hannah Maria Clay, Mary Sturman, Edward Sturman, Walter Sturman, Adelaide Clay/Starkey, Annie Clay/Jones, Henry Sturman, Lavinia and Frank Sturman, Charles Sturman and Grandmother Jackson. *(Margaret Carter)*

Mrs Sarah Patrick, a shop-keeper in Malt Mill Lane, examines a hamper she has won in a competition, early 1940s. *(Margaret Patrick)*

The wedding of the Revd Albert Cole and Laura Annie Hobbs (daughter of Henry Hobbs), which took place at High Street Methodist Church on 14 July 1917. Albert was serving as a Primitive Methodist minister at Highley in Shropshire. They are seen here in the garden of Regis House, Causeway, and the spire of Birmingham Road Methodist Church can be seen on the skyline. The party consists of, left to right, Irene Smith, the Revd William T. Cole, Mary Hobbs, John Smith, Albert Cole, Laura Hobbs, Fred Hobbs, Emily Hobbs, the Revd Arthur Wilkes and Lilian Hobbs. *(Maisie Hayman)*

Arthur John Barker was born in 1887 in Rowley village and lived for most of his life in Blackheath. He was Mayor of Rowley Regis in 1955–6, and as a widower chose Doris, his daughter-in-law, to serve as Mayoress. While on the council he served on many committees representing both Rowley Regis and Staffordshire County Council. He was made an Honorary Freeman of the Borough on 26 June 1965. *(Doris Barker)*

This soldier is named as Bill Clift, and details on the reverse of the picture indicate that he lived at 19 Blandfield Road, Blackheath. *(Eunice Dudley)*

George Newman, who lived in Oldbury Road, is seen in his uniform as a member of Blackheath Salvation Army, *c.* 1900. The family state that in his early life he was a heavy drinker, but was persuaded by the Salvation Army to turn over a new leaf. He became a changed man in later years. *(Morris Newman)*

Some of the residents of top of High Street gather for an unknown occasion in the garden of Ben Hobbs in Causeway, early 1950s. *(Margaret Green)*

As part of the celebrations for Infant Welfare Week in July 1928 there was a competition for the best decorated prams, and here we see some of the mothers and babies all decked out on their way to be judged. *(Author's Collection)*

The wedding party of Frank Percival Gaunt and Florence Dora Cooper, which took place at St Paul's Church on 28 July 1907. At the time of the wedding Percival was still working as a carpenter, as he was still to found the undertaking business for which the family has become famous. Here we see, left to right, Decimus Gaunt, Frank Percival Gaunt, Florence Cooper, Laurence Gaunt, Olive Gaunt, William Gaunt, Phoebe Gaunt, Dora Gaunt, Alan Gaunt, Gladys Gaunt and Daisy Gaunt. *(Betty Johnson)*

The Everton family with a splendid example of their coach building, in Woodland Road, at the rear entrance to their garage premises in Long Lane. They are, left to right, Frank, Sidney, Fred, Herbert and Eli, with young Ken seated inside the coach. *(Robert Everton)*

A later photograph of Evertons Garage from the front entrance in Long Lane, taken from Southwick Road. *(Robert Everton)*

Four of the railway workers from Rowley Regis and Blackheath station, early twentieth century. *(Black Country Living Museum)*

Once a well-known character who, during the run-up to Christmas, visited the various shops in the High Street area, his identity seems to have slipped from the records – as indeed may seem fitting to retain the mystery felt by the children of the town on meeting Father Christmas. *(Author's Collection)*

Tommy Smart, the Aston Villa and England player in the army in India during the First World War. He was known to issue a blood-curdling war cry when descending on opposing players, and it is believed he picked this up while on active service. *(Paul Jameson)*

Gladys Slater, a well-known Blackheath
soprano, who performed at venues across the
Midlands, in a picture taken at Christmas
1938. *(Rita Box)*

Four unidentified gentlemen from
Blackheath who have taken the latest
motorcycle and sidecar into the studio
to be recorded for posterity, 1930s.
(Eunice Dudley)

Mrs Maria Willetts (née Darby) from the sweet shop in High Street poses for this formal photograph in her best fur wrap, *c. 1930. (Dorothy Parkes)*

Widow Annie Clay with her daughter Mary
Maria Matthews Clay, *c.* 1903. *(Margaret Carter)*

May Gaunt from Powke Lane is pictured in the
uniform of the Auxiliary Fire Service in which
she served during the Second World War.
(May Botfield)

Like most towns that held their own carnivals Blackheath elected an annual Carnival Queen, and in the early 1920s Miss Enid George held the title. *(Author's Collection)*

7

Miscellaneous Events

A large crowd gathers in the car park of the George & Dragon public house in High Street to wait for the results of a prize raffle draw. The picture dates from the Second World War. (*Author's Collection*)

While delivering bread to customers in New England something spooked the horse, which bolted, and as a result Honeysett's wagon overturned in Long Lane scattering the goods all over the road and attracting a large crowd of onlookers. *(Ernest Honeysett)*

The aftermath of an accident in which Bird's fruit and vegetable lorry collided with a private car in Powke Lane. *(Malcolm Whithouse)*

Large crowds assembled in Halesowen Street to mark the opening of Carter's Electronic's first major shop, before they moved to their premises in High Street, 1965. They had come to pay their respects to their current heartthrob, Len Fairclough of *Coronation Street*, and to seek his autograph. *(Gordon Carter)*

In common with people throughout the land, the residents of Hurst Green joined together to hold street parties to mark the coronation of the present queen. Unfortunately the weather turned inclement and the revellers had to gather inside the old Sunday School building of Hurst Green Methodist Church. *(Mary Hollis)*

Chaos resulted for several hours on the main-line rail service between Worcester and Birmingham (Snow Hill) early one morning in September 1968, when a goods train carrying coal left the rails and blocked the entrance to the tunnel. *(Ida Smith)*

During periods of substantial rainfall severe flooding often occurred, with water running from Quinton and settling in the lowest point, in this case the railway line. Here we see the resulting subsidence. Workmen had to be diverted from their usual jobs to clear away the debris, and the tarpaulin at the back is believed to conceal coffins washed down the embankment from St Paul's churchyard. In the winter of 1882 the north wall of the churchyard was thrown down by a serious slip near the mouth of the railway tunnel, and the railway company rebuilt it at their own expense. *(Author's Collection)*

Once again the railway line was flooded, but this time it was caused by a 25ft trunk water main bursting in June 1960 in Vicarage Road, at one time causing a fountain of water to rise more than 10ft in the air. Most of the roadway was torn away, but as the level of the pavements had recently been raised there was no damage to most of the houses. *(Author's Collection)*

A large crowd gathered in the car park of the George & Dragon in 1949 to see the exhibits when Beaumont's brought, among other items, a stuffed whale. *(Gordon Parsons)*

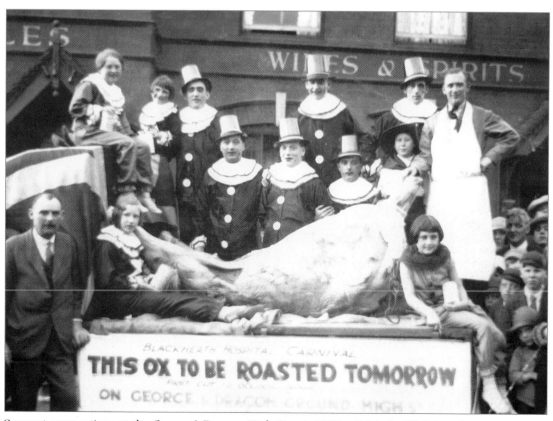

Ox roast preparations at the George & Dragon, High Street, 1920s. *(Malcolm Whitehouse)*

Residents of Shepherds Fold take to the open air to celebrate the coronation of George VI in 1937. (*Author's Collection*)

Some of the helpers are seen in the balcony of Birmingham Road Methodist Sunday School at the Sons of Rest Christmas meal, *c.* 1955. (*Frank Wyle*)

Festivities were held in Blackheath to mark coronation year in June 1911. This is a typical float which took part in the procession that was headed by the Blackheath Prize Band. On the right is Mr George Bennett, and among the group are Messrs Walker, Parish and Tom Bennett. *(Author's Collection)*

Another party dressed up for the Blackheath Carnival fancy dress parade, with Tommy Smart at the extreme right, 1930s. *(Paul Jameson)*

There was a fire at the Regis Brick Company in Station Road in about 1937, during which all the drying sheds were burnt out. They were rebuilt, but never again attained full production. Shortly afterwards the Ministry of Food took over the sheds for the storage of tinned food. Production re-started in 1945–6 when eighteen Italian prisoners-of-war were taken on to do the manual work; the sheds closed down in 1965. At the peak of production they employed between thirty and forty people, with Enoch Hobbs acting as manager after the death of his father, Benjamin, in 1942. *(Robert Hobbs)*

During the 1960s the *Birmingham Post & Mail* opened a branch office, including a small printing department, in the Market Place, Blackheath, before moving into larger premises in High Street. The official opening ceremony was performed in the presence of the Mayors of Rowley Regis and Halesowen. *(David Eades)*

Five Methodist churches joined together to form the new Blackheath Central Methodist Church, which was built on the site of the former High Street Church, and on Thursday 26 July 2001 a ceremony was held to cut the first sod. A large crowd assembled (upper picture) including representatives of other churches and town traders, to witness Councillor Bob Price (Deputy Mayor of Sandwell and former Sunday School scholar at Birmingham Road), the Revd Richard Wilde (Superintendent Minister) and Sylvia Heal (MP for Rowley Regis and Halesowen and Deputy Speaker) symbolically lift the first spade-full of earth. (*Anthony Page*)

The decorated float entered by Bird's fruit and vegetable shop, outside their High Street premises, for one of the Blackheath Carnivals in the 1920s. *(Malcolm Whitehouse)*

Members of Blackheath Orchestral Society are seen in rehearsal at a garden fete held in Solihull, mid-1950s. *(Joan Keightley)*

The winning darts team from the Yew Tree Inn, Carnegie Road, 1947–8. *(Margaret Owen)*

A Coombs Wood Operatic Society production, with Pearl Glaze on the extreme right, late 1920s. *(Ernest Honeysett)*

The Charter Mayor and Mayoress of Rowley Regis, Alderman and Mrs Ben Hobbs, are seen entering High Street Methodist Church, flanked by members of the constabulary, for what was probably Civic Sunday, *c.* 1935. The business premises owned by Mr Hobbs make a backdrop to the picture. *(Maisie Hayman)*

Joining with the rest of the nation, John Tooth, Builders Merchants, have decorated their shop window to celebrate the wedding of the Prince and Princess of Wales in 1983. *(John Tooth)*

Civic dignitaries pose with a lorry encouraging the folk of Blackheath and Rowley to engage in what today we would call recycling, to aid the war effort. The Mayor is the Revd Herbert Card, Vicar of St Giles. *(John Nightingale)*

Stalwart members of the Blackheath Conservative Club, many of them local businessmen, line up for the camera. Back row, left to right: D. Crumpton, J. Bird, T. Hackett, D. Gadd, W. Bell, D. Hackett, A. Crumpton, D. Massey, -?-. Front row: B. Moore, ? Shakespeare, T. Lench, R. Bird, W.G. Holmes. *(Leslie Bird)*

ACKNOWLEDGEMENTS

T hanks are liberally expressed to all those people, from the immediate district as well as abroad, who have raided family albums, kitchen drawers and attics to provide the pictures, as well as those who have helped to identify the people and the occasions. As before I am particularly grateful to Sandwell Community History and Archives Service (CHAS), the *Black Country Bugle* and the *County Express* for their willingness to share their collections.

Decked out in the latest fashions, the mothers of the Hill and Cakemore area proudly bring their infants and toddlers to the weekly session of the clinic in the schoolroom of the Congregational church in Green Lane, July 1930. Nurse O'Grady is seen holding a toddler at the right of the picture. The pipe in the centre is the chimney of the large heating stove which occupied the middle of the room. (*Author's Collection*)